Usborne STEM

TECHNOLOGY
Scribble Book

THE TECHNOLOGY IN THIS BOOK WAS SCRIBBLED BY:

Soraya Stafford - Davies

Written by
**ALICE JAMES &
TOM MUMBRAY**

Illustrated by
PETRA BAAN

Designed by
Emily Barden

Series editor **Rosie Dickins**

Series designer **Zoe Wray**

Expert advice from
Dr. David Rooney

CONTENTS

Write messages in machine code.

Build a landscape for a video game.

Invent a character using motion capture technology.

Think up new sources of power.

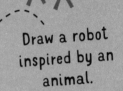

SCUTTLE

Draw a robot inspired by an animal.

Find your way through a maze to get hidden crypto-coins.

WHAT IS TECHNOLOGY?

Technology means using what we know to CREATE and BUILD anything, from wheels and bridges to robots and drones. It's about SOLVING PROBLEMS – whether by inventing a NEW solution, or finding a BETTER way of doing something.

Here are just some examples of the technology you might see around you every day.

4

WHAT'S IN THIS BOOK?

This book is full of things to:

DESIGN

SOL VE

CREATE

INVENT

EXPLORE

THINK

Technology is a really fast-moving area, and some developments are controversial – with people arguing whether or not to use them. Look at the tech in this book as you do the activities, and see if you think it's GOOD, BAD, or in between.

WHAT WILL YOU NEED?

Mostly you will only need this book and a pencil. Occasionally you might need paper, glue, a ruler and scissors.

USBORNE QUICKLINKS

To download copies of the templates in this book, and for links to inspiring websites about technology today, go to **www.usborne.com/quicklinks** and type in the keywords: 'scribble technology'.

THE NEXT BIG IDEA

Technology is all about MAKING THINGS POSSIBLE.

What sort of technology do you want to invent?
Try one of these examples, or think of your own.

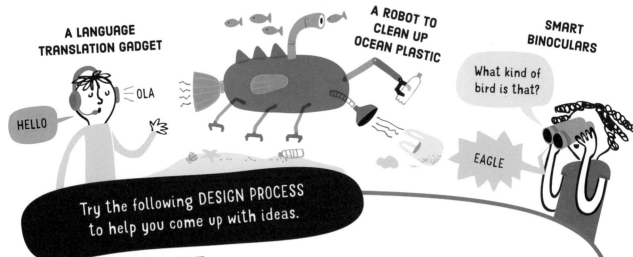

A LANGUAGE TRANSLATION GADGET

HELLO

OLA

A ROBOT TO CLEAN UP OCEAN PLASTIC

SMART BINOCULARS

What kind of bird is that?

EAGLE

Try the following DESIGN PROCESS to help you come up with ideas.

WHAT ARE THE PROBLEMS?

Start by working out WHAT problems you need to tackle. This is known as PROBLEM DEFINITION.

Create a mindmap for your chosen problem. FOR EXAMPLE:

Robot ocean cleaner problems

How will it catch plastic?

How will it move around?

FIND SOLUTIONS

Think of ways your technology could solve those problems. This is known as CONCEPTUALIZATION.

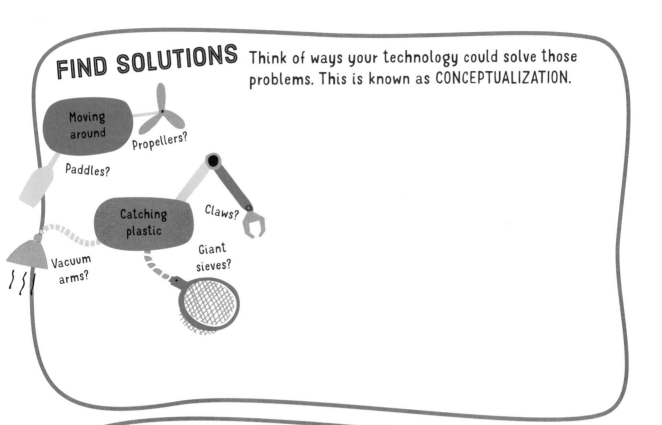

Moving around

Propellers?

Paddles?

Catching plastic

Claws?

Giant sieves?

Vacuum arms?

DESIGN IT

DRAW OUT your technology here. Add labels to show what each part does.

ROOM FOR IMPROVEMENT

Technology isn't always about coming up with a brand new idea.
Often, it's to do with DEVELOPING and IMPROVING things that already exist
or COMBINING technologies to make something better. Here are some
examples of technology that could be improved...

Cars that POLLUTE

Packaging that's NOT REUSABLE

Uh-oh...

Gadgets that RUN OUT OF BATTERY

Pick one of the examples above,
or think of your own. Follow this development
process to try to improve it.

WHAT'S BEEN TRIED BEFORE?

Think about improvements that have already
been made to try and solve the problem.

Making packaging REUSABLE

Strong fabric bag

Sturdy washable cups

ANALYZE IT

Scribble down the STRENGTHS and WEAKNESSES of the existing technology, and try to think of IMPROVEMENTS.

For example:
REUSABLE CUP

STRENGTHS
Reduces waste

WEAKNESSES
Have to remember
to bring it

IMPROVEMENT
Reusable cup that
people can wear
when not in use

Reusable
cup bangle

DESIGN IT

Design your improved
piece of technology below.

Cable network

Lots of technology relies on the INTERNET – a huge NETWORK of computers joined up by cables, most of which lie deep under the sea. The cable network looks a little like this...

CANADA

What's the fastest route between JAPAN and GREENLAND, using the FEWEST cables? Draw over the fastest route. How many cables long is it?

JAPAN

INDIA

Computers share information by sending data and images broken up into small units called PACKETS (see page 18). Packets often take different routes across the network to their end point.

AUSTRALIA

NEW ZEALAND

Start here

4 packets are being sent from New Zealand to Japan, via the 4 shortest routes. Each route is 3 cables long. Find and draw over them.

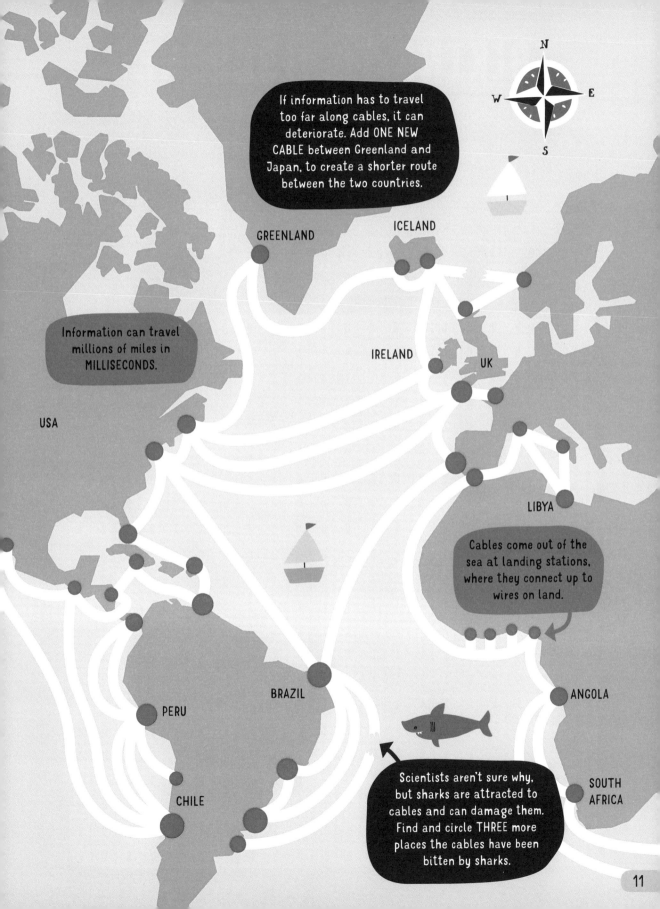

TALKING TO MACHINES

Computers work in a language called MACHINE CODE, which is made up of just two symbols – 0 and 1. The 0s and 1s represent the STATE of millions of tiny switches inside a computer's memory chips. They show whether each switch is OFF (0), or ON (1).

Each 0 or 1 is known as a BIT (short for binary digit). Bits can give the computer all sorts of information, from words to images. Shade the ON switches below to reveal an image.

```
0 0 0 0 0 0 0 0 0 0 0 0 0 0 0 0 0 0 0 0 0 0 0 0
0 0 0 0 0 0 0 1 1 1 1 1 0 0 0 0 0 0 0 0 0 0 0 0
0 0 0 0 1 1 1 1 1 1 1 1 1 1 0 0 0 0 0 0 0 0 0 0
0 0 0 1 1 1 1 1 1 1 1 1 1 1 1 1 0 0 0 0 0 0 0 0
0 0 0 1 1 1 1 0 0 0 0 1 1 1 1 0 1 0 0 0 0 0 0 0
0 0 1 1 1 1 0 0 0 0 0 0 1 1 1 1 1 0 0 0 0 0 0 0
0 0 1 1 1 1 0 0 0 0 0 0 0 1 1 1 0 0 0 0 0 0 0 0
0 1 1 1 1 0 0 0 0 0 0 0 0 0 0 0 0 0 0 0 0 0 0 0
0 1 1 1 1 0 0 1 0 0 0 0 0 0 0 1 1 0 0 0 0 0 0 0
0 1 1 1 1 0 1 1 1 0 1 0 0 0 0 0 1 1 0 0 0 0 0 0
0 1 1 1 1 1 1 1 1 1 1 1 0 1 0 0 0 1 1 0 0 0 0 0
0 1 1 1 1 1 1 1 1 1 1 1 1 1 1 0 0 0 0 1 1 0 0 0
0 1 1 1 1 1 1 1 1 1 1 1 1 1 1 1 0 0 0 1 1 0 0 0
0 1 1 1 1 1 1 1 1 1 1 1 1 1 1 1 1 0 1 1 1 0 0 0
0 1 1 1 1 1 1 1 1 1 1 1 1 1 1 1 1 1 1 1 1 1 0 0
0 1 1 1 1 1 1 1 1 1 1 1 1 1 1 1 1 1 1 1 1 0 0 0
0 1 1 1 1 1 1 1 1 1 1 1 1 1 1 1 1 1 1 0 0 0 0 0
0 0 1 1 1 1 1 0 0 0 1 1 1 1 1 0 0 0 0 0 0 0 0 0
0 0 0 1 1 1 0 0 0 0 0 1 1 1 0 0 0 0 0 0 0 0 0 0
0 0 0 1 1 1 0 0 0 0 0 1 1 1 0 0 0 0 0 0 0 0 0 0
0 0 0 1 1 1 0 0 0 0 0 1 1 1 0 0 0 0 0 0 0 0 0 0
0 0 0 1 0 1 0 0 0 0 0 1 0 1 0 0 0 0 0 0 0 0 0 0
```

When a letter is typed on a keyboard, it's converted into a set of 8 bits.
This is known as BINARY CODE.

BINARY CODE

A	01000001
B	01000010
C	01000011
D	01000100
E	01000101
F	01000110
G	01000111
H	01001000
I	01001001
J	01001010
K	01001011
L	01001100
M	01001101
N	01001110
O	01001111
P	01010000
Q	01010001
R	01010010
S	01010011
T	01010100
U	01010101
V	01010110
W	01010111
X	01011000
Y	01011001
Z	01011010

Use the key to decipher the word that's been typed here.

OFF (0)
ON (1)

Try writing 0 or 1 above each switch.

Add your own word in binary code below.
Each line is one letter.

You don't have to use all the lines.

Computer screens are made of PIXELS – tiny squares that light up different shades of red, green and blue light, mixed into over 16 MILLION COMBINATIONS.

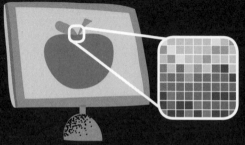

Each pixel is just ONE hue, but they're so small you barely notice them, until you look up close...

Use the pixel grid below to create your own close-up image.

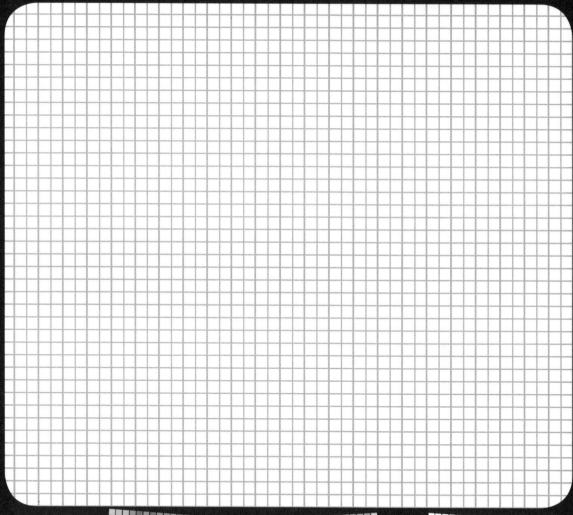

You could try...

A tree

An eye

A giraffe

ONE STEP AT A TIME

To work something out, computers need to follow precise, step-by-step instructions.
A set of instructions for a specific task is known as an ALGORITHM.

The FLOWCHART below shows an algorithm designed to sort a list of numbers into order of size.

START → Select the first number in the list.

Is the selected number (in the yellow box) larger than the next number along?

NO → Don't swap numbers → Write down order of list

YES → Swap numbers → Write down NEW order of list

Has the whole list been checked?

NO

YES → END

TRY IT YOURSELF

Use the flowchart to put this list of numbers in order from SMALLEST to BIGGEST. Each time you run through the flowchart, write the new list on the next row.

6	1	3	9	7

The yellow boxes show WHICH number you need to check each time.

This type of algorithm is known as a BUBBLE SORT...

...because the numbers 'bubble up' into the correct order.

15

GETTING AROUND

TRANSPORTATION TECHNOLOGY has been evolving for thousands of years. Vehicles have improved over time to get people to places more quickly and comfortably – whether it's down the road or to the Moon.

This timeline shows some of the BIG DEVELOPMENTS.

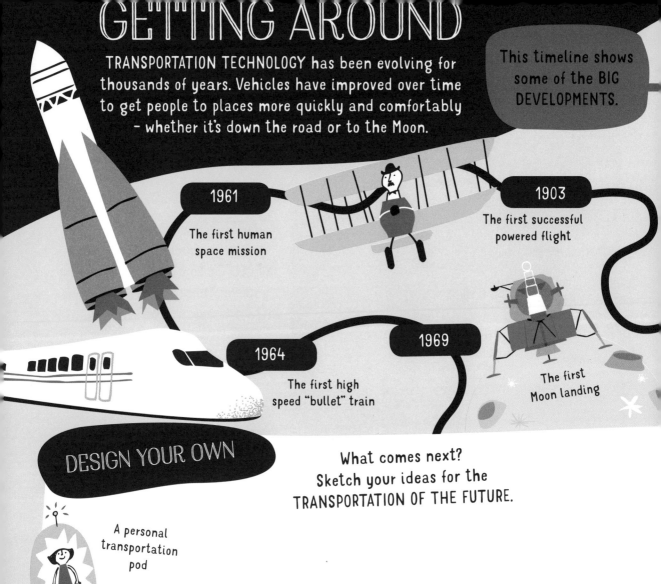

1961
The first human space mission

1903
The first successful powered flight

1964
The first high speed "bullet" train

1969
The first Moon landing

DESIGN YOUR OWN

What comes next?
Sketch your ideas for the
TRANSPORTATION OF THE FUTURE.

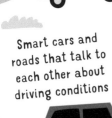

A personal transportation pod

Flying cars

Smart cars and roads that talk to each other about driving conditions

Bad traffic!

Change route...

BEEP
BEEP

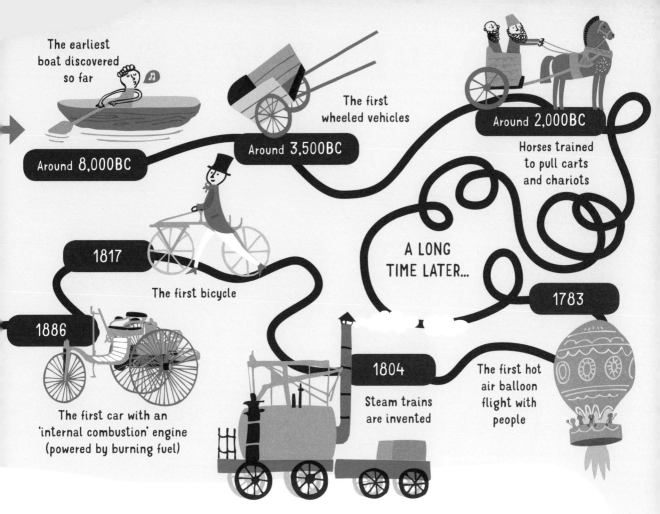

The earliest boat discovered so far

Around 8,000BC

The first wheeled vehicles

Around 3,500BC

Around 2,000BC

Horses trained to pull carts and chariots

1817

The first bicycle

A LONG TIME LATER...

1783

1886

1804

The first hot air balloon flight with people

The first car with an 'internal combustion' engine (powered by burning fuel)

Steam trains are invented

PACKET PUZZLE

The information computers send through the internet is broken up
into pieces, known as PACKETS. This means the information travels quickly,
but doesn't always arrive in the right order.

HOW IT WORKS

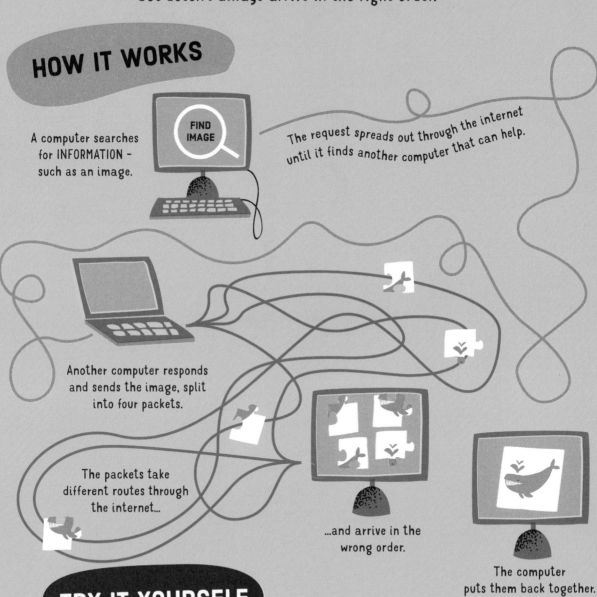

A computer searches
for INFORMATION –
such as an image.

FIND IMAGE

The request spreads out through the internet
until it finds another computer that can help.

Another computer responds
and sends the image, split
into four packets.

The packets take
different routes through
the internet...

...and arrive in the
wrong order.

The computer
puts them back together.

TRY IT YOURSELF

A computer has sent you an image split into 16 packets,
printed on the next page. Copy the template, or print it from
the Usborne QUICKLINKS website, and cut out the pieces.

Can you put them back together so that they make a whole image again?

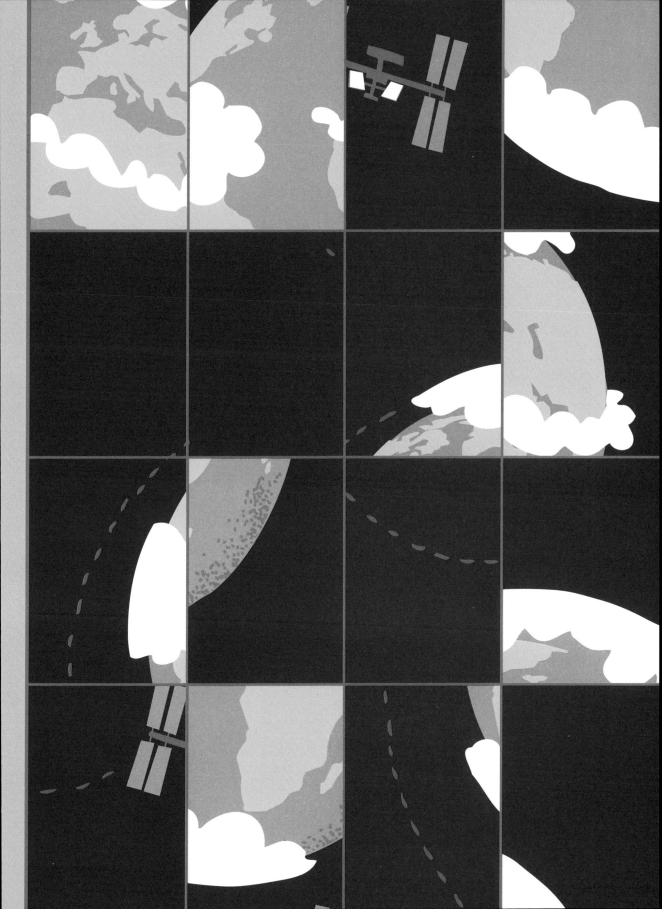

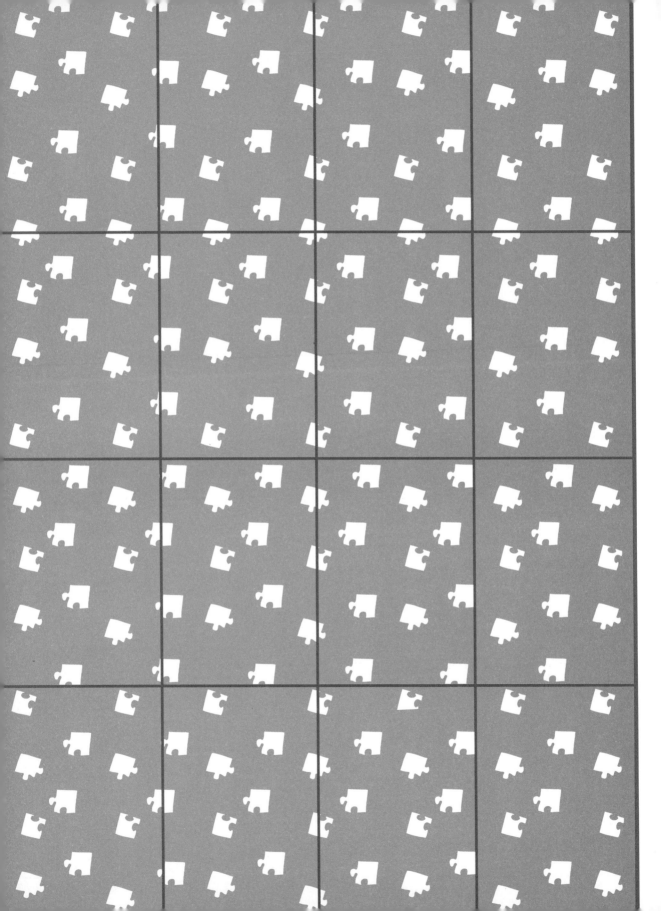

SILICON DOODLES

Inside a computer there are lots of tiny chips of silicon, printed with even tinier electronic circuits. The computer 'thinks' by sending electricity through these circuits. Chip makers who design the circuits sometimes sneak in pictures between the components.

The pictures are known as SILICON DOODLES. They're so tiny you need a microscope to see them.

DESIGN YOUR OWN
Scribble your own silicon doodles wherever you like in the white spaces between the circuits.

So far, chip makers have added all sorts of doodles, including...

...a trombone.

...an elephant wearing a cape.

...a medieval castle.

Silicon doodles used to be more common, but are becoming rarer. Unfortunately, doodles can damage circuits if misplaced by even the TINIEST distance, so many chip manufacturers don't want to take the risk.

SUPER SMART

SMART electronic devices can interact with a user or other devices. They range from smart watches which can send and receive messages, to smart speakers which understand what you say.

DESIGN YOUR OWN

Think up a new invention, where you could add smart electronics to an everyday object to make it more useful.

SCRIBBLE TO SCREEN PEN

Write anywhere and watch your drawings appear on a screen.

ANALYSIS SHOE

A smart sports shoe that sends information – including power, speed and direction – back to a computer.

NEVER–GET–LOST COAT

A coat with an in-built navigation system, which communicates with GPS satellites to help you find your way.

TURN LEFT

GIVE IT A NAME:

Auto-text

Most smart phones use a feature called AUTO-COMPLETE to suggest words or phrases as you type. It works by figuring out which words are MOST LIKELY to appear next, based on sentences you typed in the past.

For example if you typed HAPPY, you would probably see suggestions such as

In auto-complete, words are given a certain PROBABILITY of coming after other words. The probability ranges from 0 (meaning that word definitely won't appear), to 1 (meaning it definitely will).

This tool is known as a MARKOV CHAIN.

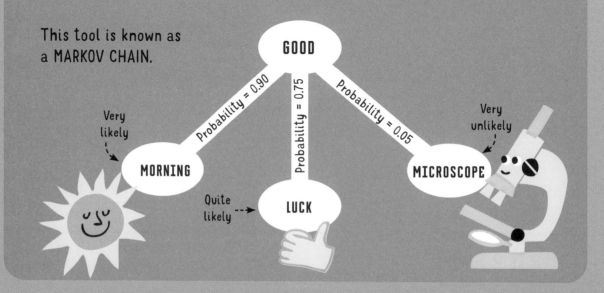

GOOD

Probability = 0.90

Probability = 0.75

Probability = 0.05

Very likely → MORNING

Quite likely → LUCK

Very unlikely → MICROSCOPE

Draw a line between words with the HIGHEST PROBABILITY each time to find the MOST LIKELY text message. Write it out here.

Now can you find the LEAST LIKELY text message, choosing the word with the LOWEST probability each time?

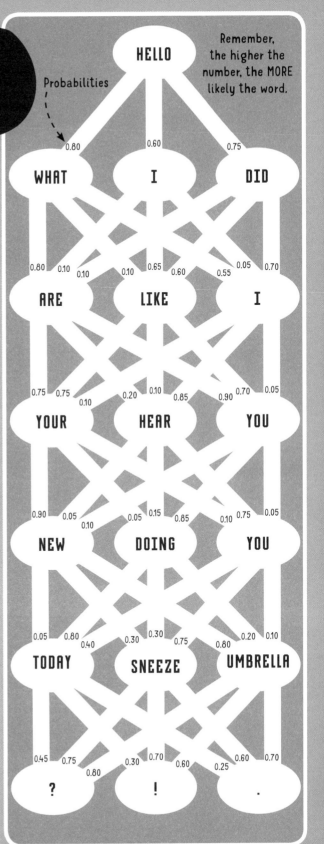

Remember, the higher the number, the MORE likely the word.

Probabilities

HELLO

0.80   0.60   0.75

WHAT   I   DID

0.80 0.10 0.10   0.10 0.65 0.60   0.55 0.05 0.70

ARE   LIKE   I

0.75 0.75 0.10   0.20 0.10 0.85   0.90 0.70 0.05

YOUR   HEAR   YOU

0.90 0.05 0.10   0.05 0.15 0.85   0.10 0.75 0.05

NEW   DOING   YOU

0.05 0.80 0.40   0.30 0.30 0.75   0.80 0.20 0.10

TODAY   SNEEZE   UMBRELLA

0.45 0.75 0.80   0.30 0.70 0.60   0.25 0.60 0.70

?   !   .

HUMAN HELPERS

A lot of tech companies are trying to develop ANDROIDS - robots that look and act like people. Making this kind of robot requires artificial intelligence, movement and lots of complicated mechanisms.

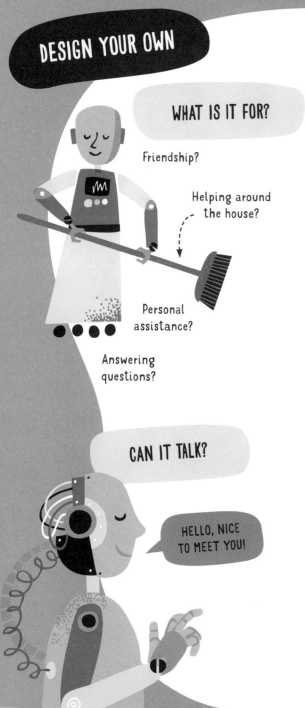

DESIGN YOUR OWN

WHAT IS IT FOR?

Friendship?

Helping around the house?

Personal assistance?

Answering questions?

CAN IT TALK?

HELLO, NICE TO MEET YOU!

HOW WILL IT GET AROUND?

Levitation?

Wheels?

Jointed legs?

Caterpillar tracks?

WILL IT LOOK LIKE A REAL PERSON?

If androids look TOO lifelike, people can find them unnerving. Scientists call this phenomenon the UNCANNY VALLEY.

WORLD BUILDER

Animators working on video games and movies use various techniques to make the things they draw look lifelike and 3-D. One technique used for computer-drawn landscapes is known as the PAINTER'S ALGORITHM.

HOW DOES IT WORK?

1. An animator uses a computer to draw everything that will appear in the landscape separately, like this...

Camels

Oasis

Sky

Trees

Dunes

2. The animator decides how the images should be layered.

3. The algorithm combines the layers into a complete landscape.

The algorithm builds a full 3-D landscape, that can be used as the setting for moving characters in complex games.

Sky

Dunes

Camels

Trees

Oasis

How were the layers ordered to make this scene? Draw or write them below.

BACK

Sky

FRONT

TRY IT YOURSELF

Use the layers below to create a landscape here.

Copy the template, or download it from the Usborne QUICKLINKS website, and cut out the shapes. Decide how you want to order the layers, then stick them in the blue box.

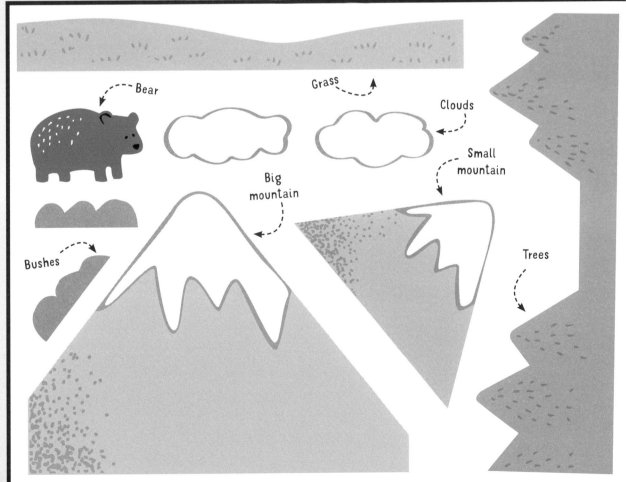

Bear

Grass

Clouds

Small mountain

Big mountain

Bushes

Trees

This technique is called the 'painter's algorithm' because it resembles the way some painters create pictures in layers.

BUT the algorithm can't handle every kind of arrangement.

How would you layer these three leaves...

...to create this?

ALL of the layers overlap, meaning there is no clear back or front. Animators have to use other algorithms to handle images like this.

GREEN SCREEN

A film technique known as GREEN SCREEN can be used to transport actors to a completely different setting.

A person is filmed in front of a giant green screen.

A computer is used to remove the green background.

Green is used because it's different from most shades of hair and skin.

ANY setting can then be put onto the scene.

Under the sea

On an alien planet

In a futuristic city

The green screen behind this actor has been removed.
Scribble in a new setting.

CAPTURING MOTION

MOTION CAPTURE is a film technique that uses actors' movements to create lifelike animations. It can be used to create scenes which would be impossible or dangerous to film otherwise.

HOW DOES IT WORK?

An actor wears a MOTION CAPTURE SUIT covered in sensors which look like ping-pong balls.

There are normally 16 sensors, positioned on the body like this.

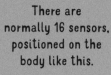
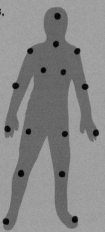

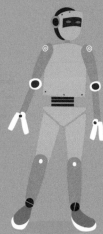

Cameras track the sensors from multiple angles as an actor moves.

A computer uses the information to create a moving 3-D figure.

An animator then designs and creates a character on top that moves naturally.

Add 16 dots to this motion capture suit to show where the sensors would be.

Use the sensors as a guide to finish off this 3-D figure.

BRING IT TO LIFE

Now you've got a 3-D figure, you can create your character. Scribble over the figure below.

IT COULD BE...

...a troll in a fantasy movie

...an alien in a science fiction TV show

...a monster from a video game

DRONE DESIGN

Flying vehicles that don't have a pilot on board are known as DRONES. They can be flown by people on the ground, or by onboard computers. This makes them perfect for dangerous jobs in hard-to-reach areas.

Camera

Drones can carry different attachments, depending on the job they need to do.

The drone below is being sent to explore a **VOLCANO**. Scribble on some useful attachments.

YOU COULD ADD...

Sensors to identify any gases being emitted?

A container to scoop up samples?

A thermometer?

HOT°

...OR ANYTHING ELSE YOU CAN THINK OF.

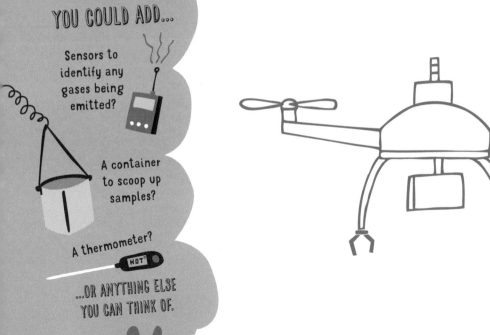

This drone is being used to help people after an EARTHQUAKE. What attachments could it have?

Flares to show rescuers where to go?

Emergency medical supplies?

A fire extinguisher?

...OR OTHER THINGS YOU THINK WOULD HELP.

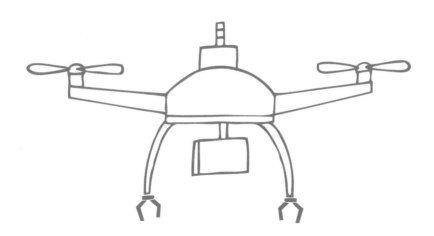

Internet of things

Many everyday devices can now be connected to the INTERNET OF THINGS - a network of devices that can talk to each other over the internet.

For example...

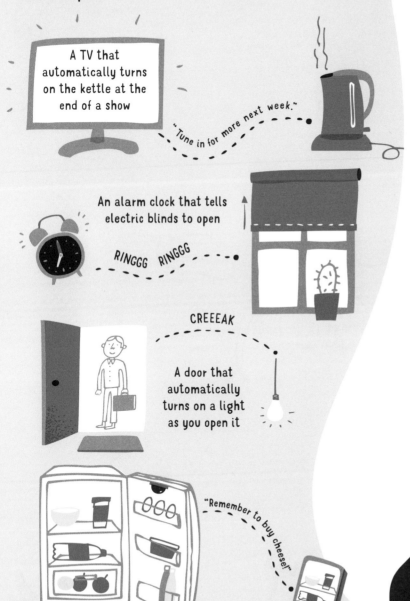

A TV that automatically turns on the kettle at the end of a show

"Tune in for more next week."

An alarm clock that tells electric blinds to open

RINGGG RINGGG

CREEEAK

A door that automatically turns on a light as you open it

"Remember to buy cheese!"

A refrigerator that can send a picture of its contents to your smartphone, so you know what food to buy

Design your own clever devices to connect to the internet of things.

What will your
devices do?

How will you control your
devices? With an app?
From a computer?
With your voice?

Will your devices need
a screen? Buttons?
Sensors? A timer?

IMPROVED REALITY

In one type of tech, known as AUGMENTED REALITY (AR), information or images from the internet are ADDED to a view of the real world through a camera or sensor. The added elements are DIGITAL, but look as if they're really there.

Some AR is really useful. This plane's front window shows key flight information.

Some AR is just for fun. This is an interactive scavenger hunt game on a phone.

Wind speed

Speed

Temperature

Cruising altitude

Which AR device could help each person here?
Draw lines to match them up.

A car window that shows live traffic information

Goggles that show where faults might be in an engine

Now open!

A smartphone map that shows landmarks, opening hours, and gives directions in different languages

A tourist exploring a new country

FRUIT TRUCK

A trucker planning the fastest routes for deliveries

A mechanic fixing a vehicle

38

AR goggles can give lots of information at a glance.
The goggles below were designed for a scuba diver.

Depth

Water temperature

Time

This shows how full the diver's oxygen tank is.

15m

23°C [73°F]

14:35

81%

This mini map lets the diver know roughly where they are, in case they drift.

Hammerhead shark

This gives an indication of animals common in the area, so the diver knows what to look for.

Design a pair of AR goggles for someone. What are they doing, and what information would be helpful? Draw the view through the goggles, and add all the useful information they need.

HOW ABOUT...

A cyclist's helmet – showing maps, traffic and road conditions?

A snowboarder's goggles – showing mountain conditions, maps and speed?

An astronaut's mask – showing temperature, location and nearby asteroids?

3-D printing

3-D printers produce SOLID STRUCTURES by printing in LAYERS.
The layers build up on top of each other until the 3-D structure emerges.

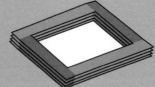

TRY IT YOURSELF
Build a picture frame layer by layer, like a 3-D printer.

Copy the template on the right or download it from Usborne QUICKLINKS.

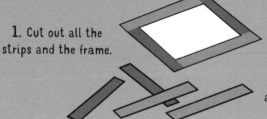

1. Cut out all the strips and the frame.

2. Build your frame, sticking on one strip at a time. Keep adding layers, gluing one on top of another, until all the strips are used up.

3-D printing technology is particularly useful for objects which need to be custom made. Scribble something you think could be 3-D printed.

Artificial limbs for people and animals, with exactly the RIGHT FIT

New tools for astronauts IN SPACE

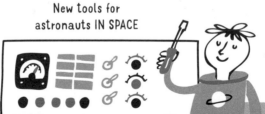

Replacement organs printed with real LIVING CELLS

PICTURE FRAME
Find or draw a picture to go in the middle before you start sticking.

Stick the blue strips along the blue sides...

...and the red strips along the red sides.

ECO TECH

Many people want to develop technology that HELPS THE PLANET,
by making the way we live less damaging, less polluting
and less wasteful. This is known as ECOTECHNOLOGY.

DESIGN a fantasy house, with lots of features and
technology to make it as ECO-FRIENDLY as you can.
There are some ideas below to get you started.

Think of a way to collect water to use again.

A bucket for rainwater

Recycle dish water

Add a space to grow things to eat.

Include one of these ways of generating your own power.

Wind turbines

A water wheel

Solar panels

PEOPLE POWER

People are WALKING, TALKING energy machines, but most of the time that energy is just wasted. Scientists are coming up with new technology to try to HARNESS energy from the way people live their lives.

Here are some people-powered sources of energy that scientists are exploring.

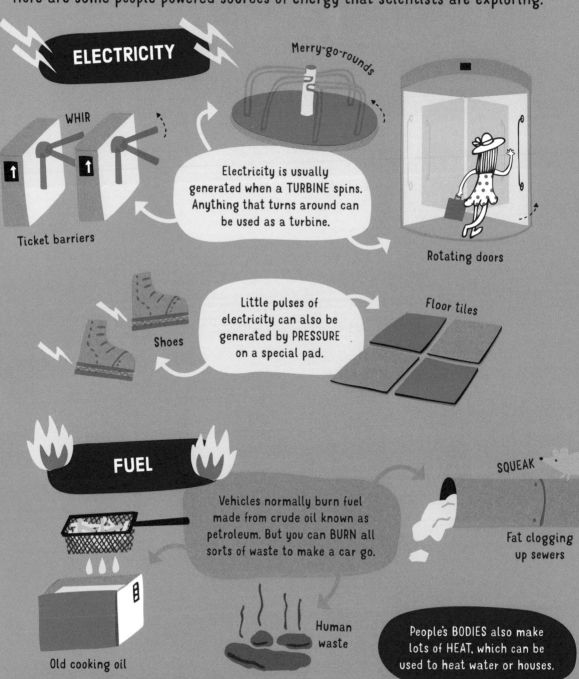

ELECTRICITY

Merry-go-rounds

WHIR

Electricity is usually generated when a TURBINE spins. Anything that turns around can be used as a turbine.

Ticket barriers

Rotating doors

Little pulses of electricity can also be generated by PRESSURE on a special pad.

Shoes

Floor tiles

FUEL

SQUEAK

Vehicles normally burn fuel made from crude oil known as petroleum. But you can BURN all sorts of waste to make a car go.

Fat clogging up sewers

Old cooking oil

Human waste

People's BODIES also make lots of HEAT, which can be used to heat water or houses.

Scribble your own ideas for technology that could generate electricity from your everyday life.

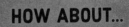

HOW ABOUT...

An exercise bike that powers a TV as you pedal.

A trampoline that generates little pulses of electricity each time you bounce.

Burning restaurant leftovers to power an oven.

BOING

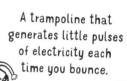

Data mining

Websites store information, or DATA, about what you click on, watch and buy. They can then study that information, in a process known as DATA MINING, and use the results to decide what else to show you.

A website that plays TV shows learns about its users, storing data about what they watch. Use the mined data on the right to work out which of these shows the site should recommend to each user.

This type of process is known as a DECISION TREE, because it splits data into lots of branches.

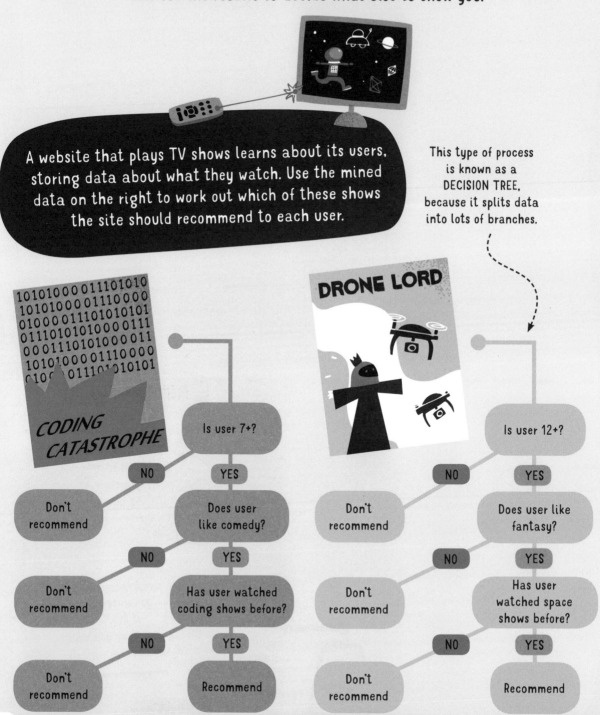

CODING CATASTROPHE

Is user 7+?
- NO → Don't recommend
- YES → Does user like comedy?
  - NO → Don't recommend
  - YES → Has user watched coding shows before?
    - NO → Don't recommend
    - YES → Recommend

DRONE LORD

Is user 12+?
- NO → Don't recommend
- YES → Does user like fantasy?
  - NO → Don't recommend
  - YES → Has user watched space shows before?
    - NO → Don't recommend
    - YES → Recommend

KIM

AGE: 12
LIKES: Fantasy, Comedy
MOST WATCHED: Space shows

RECOMMEND: _ _ _ _ _ _ _ _ _ _ _ _ _ _ _

ALEX

AGE: 8
LIKES: Cartoons, Fantasy, Sci-fi
MOST WATCHED: Coding shows

RECOMMEND: _ _ _ _ _ _ _ _ _ _ _ _ _ _ _

ANDIE

AGE: 13
LIKES: Cartoons, Sci-fi
MOST WATCHED: Robot shows

RECOMMEND: _ _ _ _ _ _ _ _ _ _ _ _ _ _ _

SAM

AGE: 7
LIKES: Sci-fi, Comedy, Fantasy
MOST WATCHED: Coding shows

RECOMMEND: _ _ _ _ _ _ _ _ _ _ _ _ _ _ _

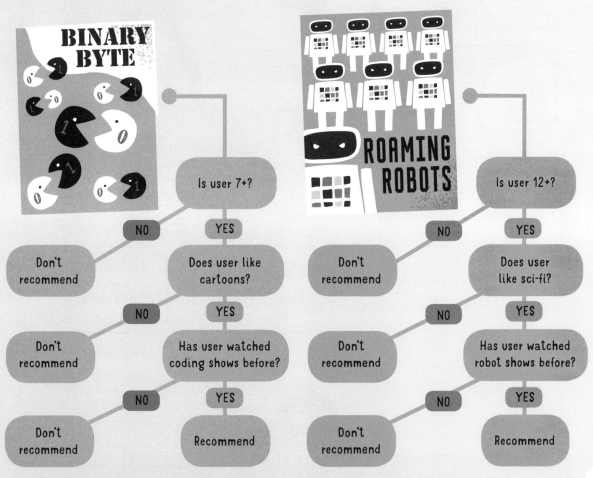

BINARY BYTE

Is user 7+?

NO — Don't recommend

YES — Does user like cartoons?

NO — Don't recommend

YES — Has user watched coding shows before?

NO — Don't recommend

YES — Recommend

ROAMING ROBOTS

Is user 12+?

NO — Don't recommend

YES — Does user like sci-fi?

NO — Don't recommend

YES — Has user watched robot shows before?

NO — Don't recommend

YES — Recommend

LOGGING YOUR LIFE

Some WEARABLE TECHNOLOGY can SENSE, TRACK and MONITOR your HEALTH, in a process known as life logging. It does this using equipment such as cameras, motion sensors, thermometers and heart-rate monitors.

Heart rate

Hours of sleep

Amount of physical activity

Temperature

Hormone levels

This surfer has a WATCH that's logging her day.

Hormones such as CORTISOL and ADRENALINE can show stress levels.

Look at the data readings from three people's life-logging technology. Which data comes from which person? Draw lines to match them up.

HEART RATE:
150 beats per minute (bpm) - VERY FAST
TEMPERATURE:
38°C (100°F) - HOT

SLEEPING HOURS: 15
BODY TEMPERATURE:
Just right 37°C (98.6°F)

ADRENALINE LEVEL:
High - SCARED
HEART RATE:
130bpm - FAST

Zzz

ARGH!

Pant Pant

DESIGN YOUR OWN WEARABLE TECH

A necklace that measures heart rate

A hat that takes a temperature

Think about WHERE the device would be worn and WHAT it would measure. Here are some ideas.

A t-shirt that analyzes sleep

Shoes that count steps

You could have one device that measures several things, or lots of separate devices.

Add your device(s) to this figure.

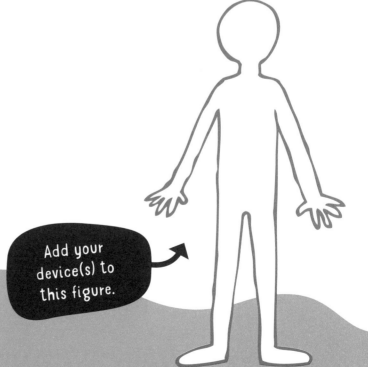

POLYGON PICTURES

To create 3-D objects in ANIMATIONS, film-makers combine lots of 2-D shapes known as POLYGONS.

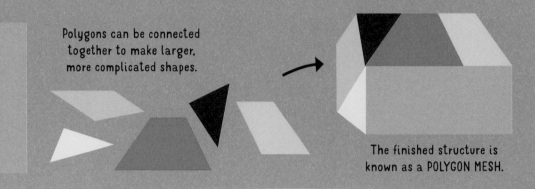

Polygons can be connected together to make larger, more complicated shapes.

The finished structure is known as a POLYGON MESH.

Connect the dots with straight lines to complete this mesh for an animated elephant. (There are lots of ways to do this.)

A computer turns the polygon mesh into an animated 3-D character or shape.

LET THERE BE LIGHT

Once the mesh is complete, a computer adds lighting effects.
A RAY-CASTING algorithm shades in each polygon automatically,
as if the mesh were a real 3-D object with a light shining at it.

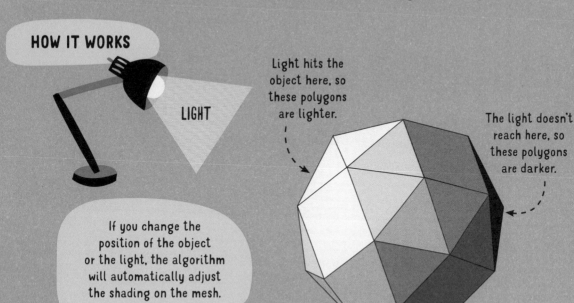

HOW IT WORKS

LIGHT

Light hits the
object here, so
these polygons
are lighter.

The light doesn't
reach here, so
these polygons
are darker.

If you change the
position of the object
or the light, the algorithm
will automatically adjust
the shading on the mesh.

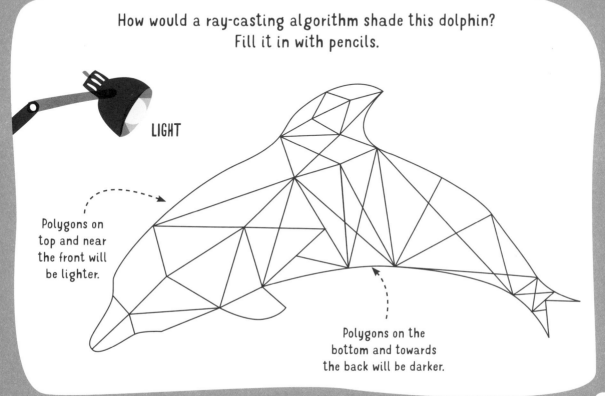

How would a ray-casting algorithm shade this dolphin?
Fill it in with pencils.

LIGHT

Polygons on
top and near
the front will
be lighter.

Polygons on the
bottom and towards
the back will be darker.

FIREWALL FILTER

Computers use the internet to communicate with each other.
Internet security guards, known as FIREWALLS, BLOCK messages that
could be used to access a computer without permission.

Here's how some firewalls work...

1 Every computer on the internet has a unique name made up of numbers, known as an IP ADDRESS.

I am **193.155.12**

193.155.12

I am **192.458.97**

192.458.97

2 These two blue computers are sending messages to the computer below, which is protected by a firewall.

3 The firewall checks the names of the senders against a list of blocked computers.

BLOCKED

192.458.97

4 **192.458.97** is on the blocked list, so no messages from it are allowed through.

FIREWALL

MESSAGE RECEIVED

190.613.48

Below, four computers are trying to send messages to a
fifth computer inside the firewall, but **TWO** are on the blocked list...

Can you complete the firewall? It can only work within the
range of the red circle. Scribble barriers inside the circle
across the routes from the blocked computers.

BLOCKED
192.613.91
193.563.65

One has
been drawn
for you.

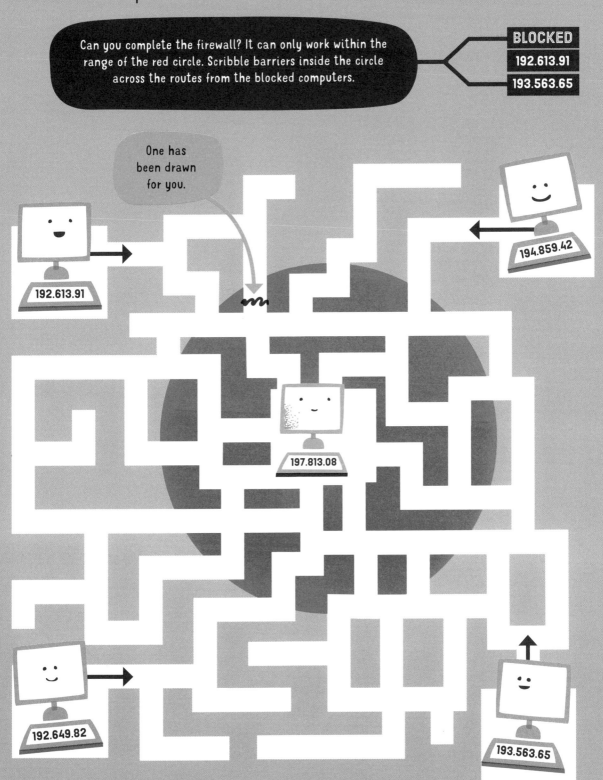

192.613.91

194.859.42

197.813.08

192.649.82

193.563.65

ROBOTS FROM NATURE

Engineers working on new robots often borrow ideas from nature. They copy the best shapes and ways of moving from animals and put it into their technology. This is known as BIOMIMICRY.

DESIGN YOUR OWN

Scribble your own animal-inspired robot. What features and skills could it have? There are ideas around the page to help you.

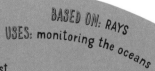

BASED ON: RAYS
USES: monitoring the oceans

Fast swimmer

Streamlined shape

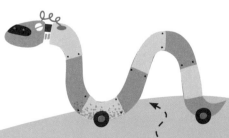

Thin, flexible body

BASED ON: SNAKES
USES: moving over different terrains

BASED ON: BEETLES
USES: search and rescue missions

Tiny, scuttling bodies

BASED ON: BIRDS
USES: scaring off pests, or taking pictures from the sky

BASED ON: GECKOS
USES: climbing walls

Sticky suction feet

YOUR ROBOT

ROBOT NAME: _

INSPIRED BY: _

SPECIAL FEATURES: _

USES: _

ENCRYPTION MISSION

Lots of payments are made over the internet, with people typing their credit card and bank details into websites. These payments have to be scrambled, or ENCRYPTED, so other people can't steal those details.

Online encryption uses a complicated set of rules to disguise numbers.

Try inventing your own rule, to encrypt the credit card numbers below.

YOUR RULE COULD BE:

- Add 3 to every digit
- Write the number backwards
- Multiply each digit by 2

For example if your rule is MULTIPLY EACH DIGIT BY 2, the number **4312** would turn into **8624**.

The more complicated a rule is, the harder it is to crack.

RULE: _____

CARD NUMBER 1: **6587 4464 2331 9677**

ENCRYPTED VERSION: _____

CARD NUMBER 2: **1363 7825 9122 3374**

ENCRYPTED VERSION: _____

Most information sent over the internet uses something known as PUBLIC KEY ENCRYPTION to keep it secure. It works like this...

A PUBLIC KEY encrypts the information, just like the rules on the previous page.

A PRIVATE KEY then unlocks the information, and turns it back into something understandable.

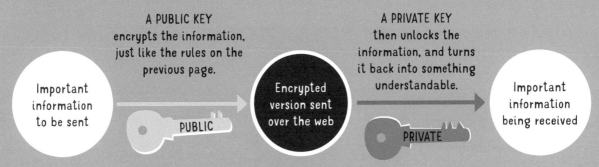

Important information to be sent

PUBLIC

Encrypted version sent over the web

PRIVATE

Important information being received

It's a little like having a padlock with a key. Anyone can use the padlock to LOCK something (that's the PUBLIC part), but only the person with the key can UNLOCK it (that's the PRIVATE part).

Here are some simple public key encryptions. Figure out and fill in the missing information or rule.

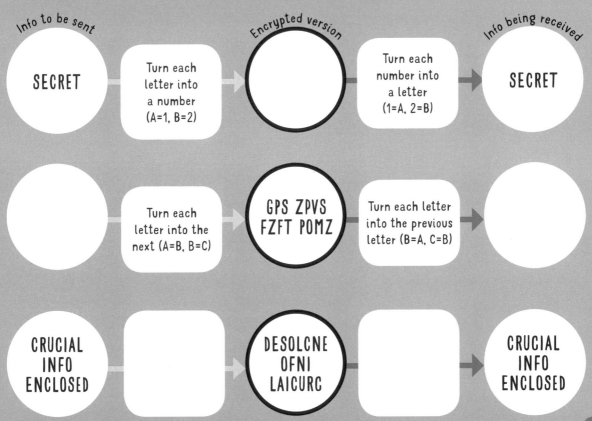

Info to be sent

Encrypted version

Info being received

SECRET

Turn each letter into a number (A=1, B=2)

Turn each number into a letter (1=A, 2=B)

SECRET

Turn each letter into the next (A=B, B=C)

GPS ZPVS FZFT POMZ

Turn each letter into the previous letter (B=A, C=B)

CRUCIAL INFO ENCLOSED

DESOLCNE OFNI LAICURC

CRUCIAL INFO ENCLOSED

57

UNCHARTED WATERS

SONAR, short for SOUND NAVIGATION AND RANGING,
can be used to measure the depth of water.

HOW SONAR WORKS

Boats beam sound
waves towards the
bottom of the sea...

...which bounce off
the ocean floor and
back to the ship.

The LONGER it takes
for the echo to return
to the surface, the
DEEPER the ocean is.

Sonar is used to create maps of the
ocean floor. Navigators use the maps,
like the one on the right, to plan
routes that are deep enough for big
ships to travel through. Different
shades represent different depths.

KEY

0-9m	
10-19m	
20-29m	
30-39m	
40-49m	

The red areas are
the shallowest.

The dark green sections
are the deepest.

This ship can ONLY
sail where the water
is 20m or deeper.

PORT A

Can you find a safe route
for the ship to follow from
Port A to Port B?

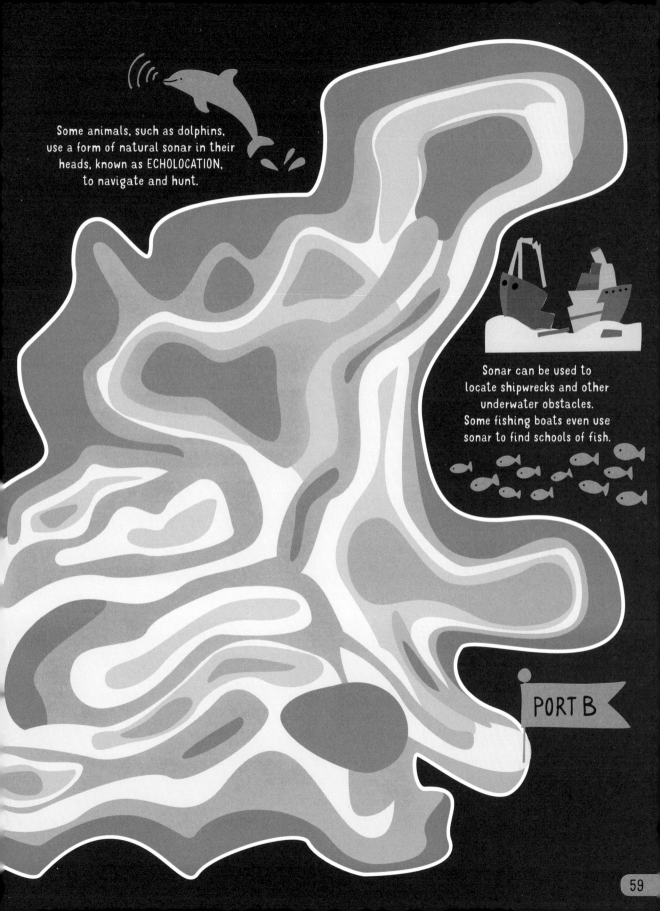

Some animals, such as dolphins, use a form of natural sonar in their heads, known as ECHOLOCATION, to navigate and hunt.

Sonar can be used to locate shipwrecks and other underwater obstacles. Some fishing boats even use sonar to find schools of fish.

PORT B

Origami tech

ORIGAMI – an ancient Japanese art of paper folding – has inspired some cutting-edge technology. An origami technique known as the MIURA FOLD, which can transform a sheet from tiny to huge, has been especially useful...

SPACE TECH

Solar panels are FOLDED for launch...

...then OPEN to catch the Sun's rays.

MEDICAL TECH

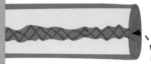
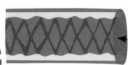

Folded mesh can slide through damaged blood vessels....

...then unfold to hold them open.

BUILD YOUR OWN

Copy the template opposite, or download it from the Usborne QUICKLINKS website, and cut along the solid line.

1. Pleat the paper along the STRAIGHT lines. Fold the BLACK lines UP and the GREEN lines DOWN, to form a strip.

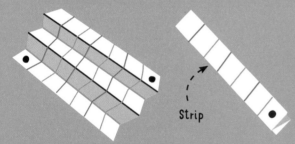

Strip

2. Next, fold your strip along each of the diagonal lines. This time, fold the RED lines UP and the BLUE lines DOWN.

3. Unfold the paper. Refold all the ZIG-ZAGS. Make the folds really crisp and sharp.

Pinch the RED zig-zags UP.

Pinch the BLUE zig-zags DOWN.

4. Fold up the paper along those zig-zags, into a small concertina.

5. Hold the two corners marked by black dots and pull them apart. Push them back together. The fold should open and close easily.

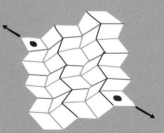

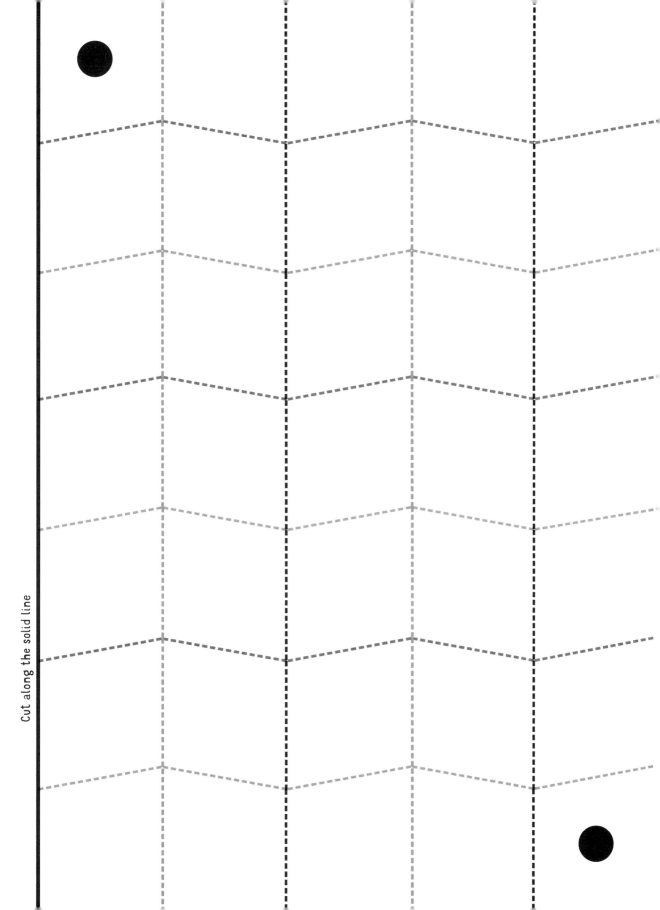

Cut along the solid line

Mining the scrapheap

Many of the metals needed to build new tech are rare and difficult to mine.
One solution is to recycle materials, known as E-WASTE, from old or
discarded electronic devices – a process known as URBAN MINING.

Here is a list of recyclable materials found in the scrapheap below.

KEY

- Silicon
- Graphite
- Cobalt
- Gold
- Copper
- Steel
- Lithium
- Plastic
- Palladium
- Nickel

Some of the materials needed to build a new smartphone include:

SMARTPHONE

Can you find them in the scrapheap below? Mark the circle of each material every time you find it in the heap.

LAPTOP

KETTLE

TABLET

HAIR DRYER

MUSIC PLAYER

WATCH

PRINTER

CONTROLLER

CAMERA

TELEVISION

The new smartphone can be made by recycling just 2 of these products – which ones?

1.

2.

63

ONLINE RICHES

CRYPTOCURRENCY is a kind of money that exists entirely ONLINE - you can't hold it in your hand, but you can buy or sell things with it on the internet. Usually, cryptocurrency 'coins' are generated by MINING - which means solving complicated puzzles on a computer, and gaining a coin as a reward.

TRY mining some imaginary CRYPTO-COINS, a little like a computer would do.

First, solve these calculations.

Use this space for scribbling your working out.

$26 + 3 + 1 - 16 =$ ⬭

$35 - 10 + 3 - 1 =$ ⬭

$5 \times 2 \times 3 =$ ⬭

$15 + 7 - 20 + 5 =$ ⬭

$3 \times 3 \times 2 =$ ⬭

$41 - 11 - 15 - 9 =$ ⬭

$121 \div 11 =$ ⬭

$36 + 3 - 20 + 4 =$ ⬭

$9 + 8 + 10 - 12 =$ ⬭

The mining process means the coins have to be earned - not magicked up. In real life the calculations are so complicated they can take super-fast computers months to solve.

Now use the answers to the calculations on the left to find a route through this mine. Mark an X on the circle where the coins are hidden.

DIG
DIG

25   14

2   16

3   29   27   30

24

17   10   4   18   7   26

5

1   22   6   32

12

13   19   11   21

23

8   9

15

SCI-FI TECH

For decades, science-fiction writers have been imagining astonishing gadgets – some of which have helped to inspire cutting-edge technology.

Read the descriptions below. Then match each piece of technology to the story that inspired it and write its letter in the white box.

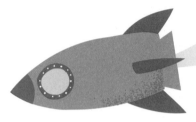

A. SPACE ROCKETS

DATE: 1889
BOOK: IN THE YEAR 2889
by Jules Verne

WHAT HAPPENS: People communicate using a machine called a phonotelephote which sends images and sounds long distances via mirrors and wires.

DATE: 1897
BOOK: WAR OF THE WORLDS
by H.G. Wells

WHAT HAPPENS: Martian invaders come to Earth in huge inter-planetary fighting machines.

B. THE WORLD WIDE WEB

DATE: 1949
BOOK: 1984
by George Orwell

WHAT HAPPENS: The government watches everyone through devices called telescreens.

BONJOUR

C. VIDEOPHONES

DATE: 1961
BOOK: DIAL 'F'
FOR FRANKENSTEIN
by Arthur C. Clarke

WHAT HAPPENS: Phones in homes all over the world link up and talk to each other in a network.

D. CCTV CAMERAS

Imagine you're writing a sci-fi novel about an interplanetary explorer, searching the galaxy for aliens. Design a gadget to help.

A sensor to detect lifeforms?

A device to translate alien languages?

X%$ 98*22!X

HELLO, EARTHLING

A new kind of spaceship?

THINKING LOGICALLY

All the information inside computers is stored as 1s and 0s.
Computer circuits process these numbers using devices known as LOGIC GATES.

Logic gates take numbers (the INPUT) and turn them into an OUTPUT,
according to a set of rules. Here are three of them – **AND**, **OR** and **NOT** gates.

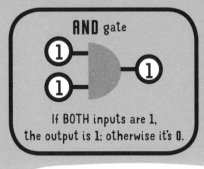

AND gate

If BOTH inputs are 1,
the output is 1; otherwise it's 0.

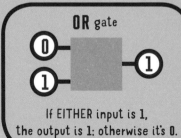

OR gate

If EITHER input is 1,
the output is 1; otherwise it's 0.

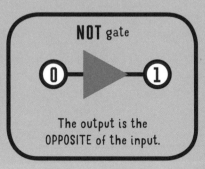

NOT gate

The output is the
OPPOSITE of the input.

Follow the circuit below
and write the output of each
logic gate in the circles.

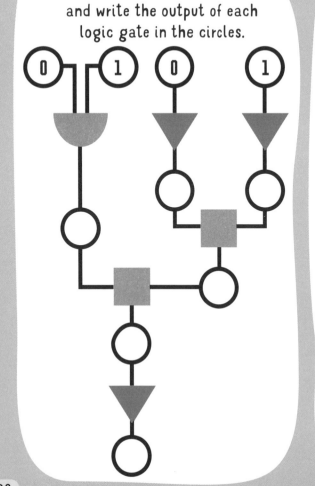

Add the missing logic
gates into this circuit.

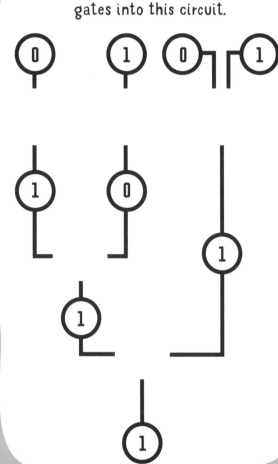

FOOD FOR THE FUTURE

BIOTECHNOLOGY is a technology that uses LIVING THINGS to solve problems.
For example, scientists can EDIT the GENES in food crops to give plants useful
properties – such as resisting diseases, surviving extreme weather, or tasting better.

WHAT ARE GENES?

Genes are the instructions that tell living things what
they will LOOK LIKE, and what PROPERTIES they will have.

Genes contain four key parts called BASES.
The bases join up in specific PAIRS.

Lots of pairs of bases together
form a long chain, known as DNA.

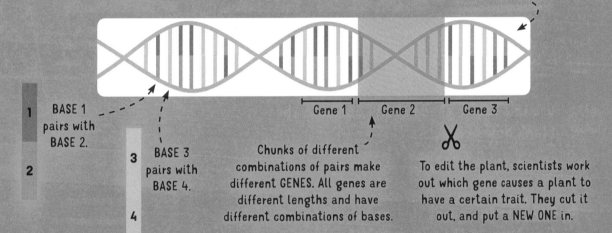

1 BASE 1 pairs with BASE 2.

2

3 BASE 3 pairs with BASE 4.

4

Gene 1   Gene 2   Gene 3

Chunks of different
combinations of pairs make
different GENES. All genes are
different lengths and have
different combinations of bases.

To edit the plant, scientists work
out which gene causes a plant to
have a certain trait. They cut it
out, and put a NEW ONE in.

Each of these crops could benefit from one of the
properties below. Put the correct letter in each box.

A DROUGHT RESISTANCE
Helps crops survive
in dry conditions

B STRONGER BRANCHES
Helps crops survive
in windy weather

C FLOOD RESISTANCE
Helps crops survive
in wet conditions

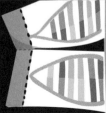

Imagine you are trying to improve a type of BANANA plant. A section of the banana's DNA is on the next page.

Copy the template on the next page, or download it from the Usborne QUICKLINKS website. Cut along the SOLID BLACK lines to cut out the DNA chain and the three blank genes.

1. Build the DNA strand.

 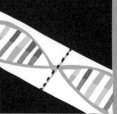

Fold along the RED dotted line so that Strand 1 faces Strand 2, and stick the two BLUE TABS together.

Fold Strand 2 back along the BLACK dotted line.

Repeat the process with Strands 2 and 3, sticking the YELLOW TABS together, to make one long DNA strand.

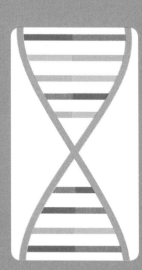

2. Use this key to shade in the bases on the blank NEW GENES.

1	2	3	4

3. Here are the genes that need editing OUT. Find them in the banana's DNA and mark them with a pencil.

This gene makes the plant **VULNERABLE TO DISEASE.**

This makes the fruit **BRUISE EASILY.**

This means the fruit contains **FEW VITAMINS.**

4. Cut out the unwanted genes and stick the new ones in the gaps.

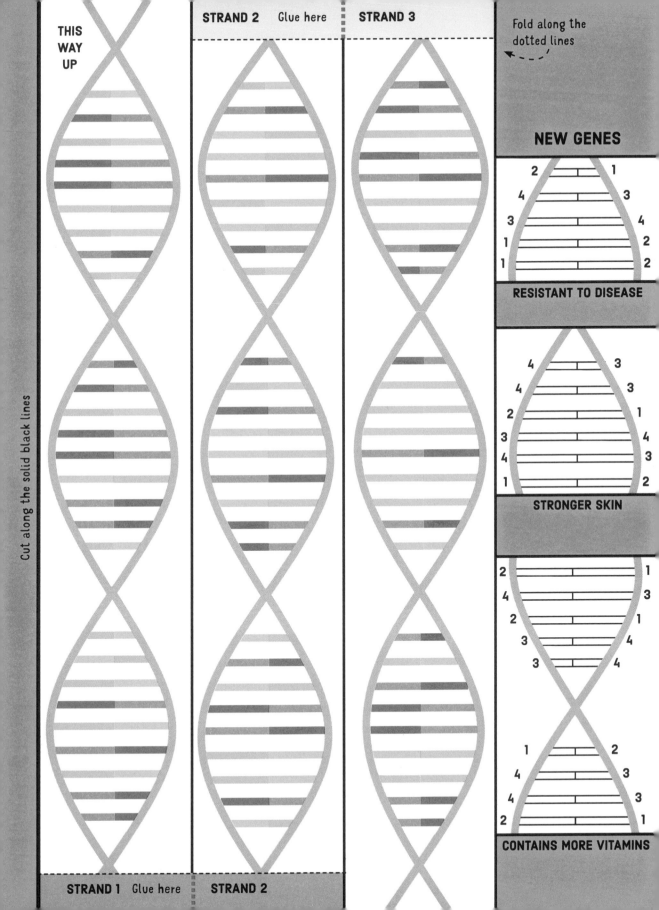

Computers of the future

Computers work using chips covered in switches. The MORE SWITCHES a chip has, the MORE INFORMATION it can handle, MORE QUICKLY. For the past 50 years, switches have been getting smaller and smaller so more of them fit on a chip.

BUT...

...it's physically impossible for switches to KEEP getting smaller.

Instead, scientists are trying to develop new ways of computing.

Researchers are currently working on these exciting NEW systems of computing.
Link each system to the correct description.

QUANTUM COMPUTING

ON   OFF   ON & OFF

A Uses LIGHT, where traditional computers use electricity. Light can carry 20 times more information than electricity.

NEUROMORPHIC COMPUTING

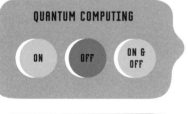

B Uses tiny SUBATOMIC PARTICLES, known as QUBITS, instead of switches. QUBITS can be on or off, or on AND off *at the same time* – so they can handle more possibilities at once.

OPTICAL COMPUTING

C Uses MULTIPLE computers to SHARE tasks.

CLOUD COMPUTING

D Mimics the way information is processed by brain cells, or NEURONS. This allows information to be handled quickly and efficiently.

THE FUTURE OF TECHNOLOGY

Technology moves extremely fast, and new developments and inventions can have a big effect on the way we live. So it's important to think about bigger questions, such as how tech fits into society, and what tech should and shouldn't be able to do.

WHAT DO YOU THINK?
Scribble some of your thoughts and ideas on these pages.

Scientists are trying to make computers more intelligent all the time. But can a computer become TOO intelligent?

What if a computer can override the instructions a person gives it?

What if it can communicate with other computers without people knowing?

Can a computer be more intelligent than a human?

Lots of jobs are now done by machines instead of people, because machines can be safer or cheaper. But are there any jobs you think should NEVER be done by machines?

Do you think machines can be CREATIVE and make good music, stories or art?

Can machines be CARING, and help the sick or elderly?

NO

MAYBE

YES

Should a machine ever be put IN CHARGE of people?

There are no right or wrong answers to these questions. Scientists, governments and the public are still debating the issues, and people's ideas are always changing.

10-11 CABLE NETWORK

The current quickest route from Japan to Greenland is marked in BLACK. It's 11 cables long.

ONE new route could be added between Japan and Greenland where the BLUE cable is.

The FOUR routes the packets take between New Zealand and Japan are marked in ORANGE, YELLOW, PINK and PURPLE.

The places the sharks have damaged are circled in RED.

12-13 TALKING TO MACHINES

Shading the ON switches reveals a dinosaur.

The typed word is QUACK.

15 ONE STEP AT A TIME

The list of numbers gets ordered like this.

1	6	3	9	7
1	3	6	9	7
1	3	6	9	7
1	3	6	7	9

18-19 PACKET PUZZLE

The finished image looks like this.

24-25 AUTO-TEXT

The MOST LIKELY sentence is:

HELLO WHAT ARE YOU DOING TODAY?

The LEAST LIKELY sentence is:

HELLO I I YOU YOU UMBRELLA!

28-30 WORLD BUILDER

The drawings were layered like this.

BACK

 SKY

 DUNES

 CAMELS

 TREES

 OASIS

FRONT

38-39 IMPROVED REALITY

46-47 DATA MINING

KIM

ALEX

ANDIE

SAM

48–49 LOGGING YOUR LIFE

SLEEPING HOURS: 15
BODY TEMPERATURE:
Just right 37°C (98.6°F)

ADRENALINE LEVEL:
High - SCARED
HEART RATE:
130bpm - FAST

HEART RATE: 150 bpm
- VERY FAST
TEMPERATURE:
38°C (100°F) - HOT

52–53 FIREWALL FILTER

Here is one solution – you may have
put them in slightly different positions.

56–57 ENCRYPTION MISSION

1. Encrypted information:
19 5 3 18 5 20

2. Original information:
FOR YOUR EYES ONLY

3. Key:
WRITTEN BACKWARDS

58–59 UNCHARTED WATERS

This is the route the ship can
take between the two ports.

63 MINING THE SCRAPHEAP

The two devices that
could be recycled to make
a new smartphone are: WATCH and CAMERA

PORT A

PORT B

64–65 ONLINE RICHES

26 + 3 + 1 − 16 = **14**

35 − 10 + 3 − 1 = **27**

5 × 2 × 3 = **30**

15 + 7 − 20 + 5 = **7**

3 × 3 × 2 = **18**

41 − 11 − 15 − 9 = **6**

121 ÷ 11 = **11**

36 + 3 − 20 + 4 = **23**

9 + 8 + 10 − 12 = **15**

The crypto-coins are at the pink circle.

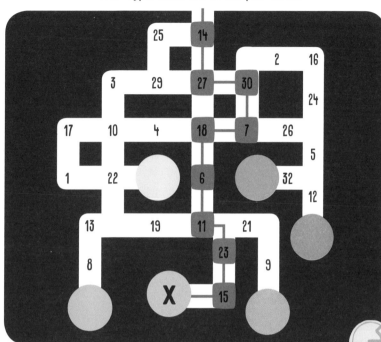

66–67 SCI-FI TECH

A. **IN THE YEAR 2889**
Videophones

B. **WAR OF THE WORLDS**
Space rockets

C. **1984**
CCTV

D. **DIAL 'F' FOR FRANKENSTEIN**
World Wide Web

68 THINKING LOGICALLY

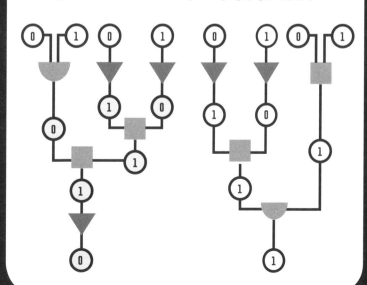

69–72 FOOD FOR THE FUTURE

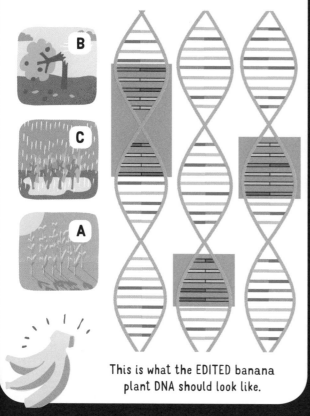

This is what the EDITED banana plant DNA should look like.

73 COMPUTERS OF THE FUTURE

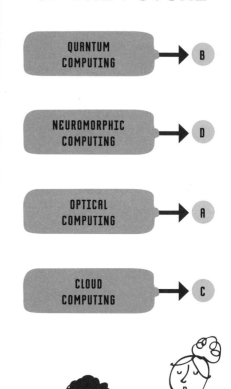

QUANTUM COMPUTING → B

NEUROMORPHIC COMPUTING → D

OPTICAL COMPUTING → A

CLOUD COMPUTING → C

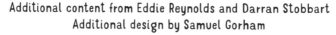

Additional content from Eddie Reynolds and Darran Stobbart
Additional design by Samuel Gorham

First published in 2019 by Usborne Publishing Ltd., Usborne House, 83-85 Saffron Hill, London EC1N 8RT, England. www.usborne.com. Copyright © 2019 Usborne Publishing Ltd.